ADHD
Attention Deficit Hyperactivity Disorder

Defining and Understanding a Diagnosis of ADHD

Susan Reed

Table of Contents

Introduction

This book will give an overview of Attention Deficit Hyperactivity Disorder, including an explanation of its subtypes, symptoms and affected demographics. It will then give an account of the history of ADHD, followed by a summary of the suspected causes of ADHD. Next, descriptions of disorders that commonly accompany ADHD will be included. Finally, descriptions of the diagnosis and treatment processes will be given.

What is ADHD?

Attention Deficit Hyperactivity Disorder, commonly known by the acronym ADHD, is a common brain disorder that affects attention and behavior. There are three different types of ADHD, which manifest themselves in slightly different ways. These sub-types of ADHD are as follows:

Predominantly inattentive ADHD:

People with the predominantly inattentive form of ADHD find their attention constantly drifting. They are frequently and easily distracted, making it difficult to concentrate on a task or learn a new skill. Following written or verbal instructions can be challenging, and there are often difficulties with processing information quickly. Sufferers tend to bore easily and spend a great deal of time daydreaming; which can cause problems at school, at work, or during social interactions. There is a tendency to misplace personal belongings and forget important dates. People with this form of the condition are often slow to complete tasks and may appear to be constantly confused, or in a dream-like state.

Predominantly hyperactive-impulsive ADHD:

People with the predominantly hyperactive form of ADHD have difficulties with controlling their behavior. Sufferers find it difficult to be patient, and often have a hard time waiting for things or sitting still. They cannot properly restrain themselves and may act impulsively, throw tantrums, make inappropriate comments, disregard the consequences of their behavior and have extremely emotional displays. There is a tendency to talk constantly, to fidget excessively and to touch or handle everything in the immediate environment. Performance at tasks that require quiet work and minimal movement, such as schoolwork or office work, may suffer.

Combined hyperactive-impulsive and inattentive ADHD:

This is the most common type of ADHD. As the name suggests, people with this form of ADHD display significant symptoms of both inattention and hyperactivity.

Between 3% and 5% of the population of North America and Europe have ADHD. Rates of diagnosis vary wildly between different countries with North America consistently reporting the highest rates of ADHD in the world. Among schoolchildren in the United States, ADHD rates have skyrocketed, and currently sit somewhere between 3% and 16%.

Boys are much more likely to be diagnosed with ADHD than girls. There are at least twice as many confirmed cases of males with ADHD than confirmed females; some estimates have found as many as four diagnosed boys to every one diagnosed girl. It is not yet known whether the gender gap is due to a genuine biological gender difference, or an erroneous difference in diagnosis rates. Preliminary studies have found that girls who display inattentive or hyperactive symptoms are far less likely than boys to be suspected of having ADHD by parents and teachers, which may account for some of the discrepancy. Sub-types of ADHD involving hyperactivity are much more prevalent among boys, while the primarily inattentive subtype tends to have a more even gender divide.

Rates of ADHD diagnosis have been steadily increasing in recent years; from 2001 to 2010 alone, the United States saw a 25% increase in ADHD, bringing the disorder from an incidence of 2.5% of the population up to 3.1%. At 3.1% of the population affected, the disorder is now considered an epidemic. The reasons for the dramatic increase are not fully understood; some mental health practitioners credit better awareness and detection strategies, while skeptics point to an overzealousness to diagnose misbehaving children with a disorder. ADHD diagnoses have been the source of considerable controversy; because there is no laboratory test or neuroimaging test that can confirm ADHD, diagnoses rest entirely on the strength of a psychologist's opinion.

Because of its vague diagnostic criteria, there have been some critics who argue that ADHD does not, in fact, exist. Retired neurologist Fred Baughman has become one the most outspoken critics of ADHD, calling the disorder a "total, 100% fraud" and publishing books and videos to that effect. A 2002 survey in the United States found that 22% of the population who had heard of ADHD did not believe it to be a real disease. Even among psychologists who do regard ADHD as a legitimate disease, there has been a great deal of criticism for the increasingly vague guidelines for ADHD diagnosis; some papers have gone so far as to call the dramatic increase in ADHD diagnoses a "false epidemic" brought on by the relaxation of symptom criteria.

Symptoms of ADHD generally begin to appear sometime before an individual's seventh birthday, although the disorder may go undiagnosed well into adulthood. It was once believed that children would naturally grow out of ADHD as they aged; research now shows that between 66% and 87% of children with ADHD still retain significant symptoms in adulthood, and 15% of them show absolutely no decrease in symptom severity with age.

ADHD is a chronic condition; there is no cure. However, many ADHD patients come up with compensation strategies as they age to overcome their disorder. People with high IQs have proven to be particularly adept at compensating for their disorder, to the extent that some people believe individuals in the 'gifted' IQ range (having an IQ of approximately 125 or higher) should be ineligible for an ADHD diagnosis.

ADHD can have devastating consequences for those afflicted with it. Despite the availability of special educational resources, only 63% of those with ADHD earn high school diplomas. The impact on college graduation is even more striking; fewer than 5% of ADHD sufferers complete post-secondary education, while approximately 28% of the general population achieves this feat. It is difficult to quantify the effects of the disorder in the workforce, but many adults with ADHD have reported suffering career setbacks, disciplinary action and even termination due to their ADHD.

Many celebrities have been diagnosed with ADHD, including Jim Carrey, Avril Lavigne, Kurt Cobain, Howie Mandel, Glenn Beck, Britney Spears, Justin Timberlake, Ty Pennington, Michael Phelps, Jamie Oliver and William "will.i.am" Adams.

History of ADHD

Although hyperactivity has been noted for hundreds of years, we find the first formal record of an ADHD-like disorder dating back to the eighteenth century. The first known record of an attention disorder comes from the 1775 medical textbook *Philosophische Arzt*, which contains an entire chapter dedicated to the subject. In the book, patients were described as being capable only of studying anything "superficially", and having a shallow understanding of a great deal of topics. The book also notes that people with attention deficits frequently displayed poor judgment due to their inability to devote the proper time and energy to the decision-making process; it goes on to suggest that these people did not take anything seriously, as their condition did not permit them to think about the possible consequences of their own actions. Treatment for people with attention deficits included isolation in a silent, dark room during times of incessant hyperactivity, and therapies involving exercise, horseback riding, steel powder, mineral waters and cold baths at other times.

Although the first two editions of *Philosophische Arzt* were published anonymously, the author is now known to be a German physician named Melchior Adam Weikard. Weikard, who would later go on to serve as the official court physician of Russian Empress Catherine II, chose to publish the textbook anonymously for fear of the Catholic Church's outrage at its anti-faith healing contents. As he predicted, the book was reviled in its time, and the discovery of attention deficit disorders went largely unnoticed.

Sir Alexander Crichton, a Scottish physician who would later go on to serve as the royal physician of the Russian Tsar

Alexander, described a condition he called "Mental Restlessness" in his 1798 book titled *An inquiry into the nature and origin of mental derangement: comprehending a concise system of the physiology and pathology of the human mind and a history of the passions and their effects.* Chrichton referred to the disorder as "a disease of attention", and made a note of how easily those with mental restlessness could be distracted by ordinary things. When questioned, his patients were said to refer to their hyperactive behavior as 'the fidgets'. Chrichton believed that children with mental restlessness should receive specialized education, as it was impossible for them to function in a regular classroom setting.

After the publication of Chricton's work, more than one hundred years lapsed without any further medical research on ADHD. No mention of the disorder, or of 'mental restless' appeared in medical publications. The disorder had not yet become part of mainstream medical practice. In fact, the next mention of an ADHD-like disorder came in the 1902 'Goulstonian lectures' delivered to London's Royal College of Physicians by Sir George Frederick Still, widely regarded as the father of pediatrics. The lectures – which were later published as articles in the world's leading medical journal, 'The Lancet' – included a segment which described forty-three children who appeared to suffer from a common set of symptoms. These children were reported to be impulsive, excessively emotional, difficult to discipline, aggressive, and incapable of attending to any sort of task, despite being of normal intelligence. Stills referred to this mysterious condition as "a defect of moral consciousness which cannot be accounted for by any fault of environment"; today, most of these children are believed to have suffered from the combined form of attention deficit hyperactivity disorder. He also noted that the condition was likely hereditary and consulted with the children's teachers to confirm that their condition was causing problems with school performance.

The next mention of ADHD symptoms found in medical literature occurred following two global epidemics. The first of these epidemics was the 1917 epidemic of Encephalitis Lethargica that gradually spread across the entire world. Commonly known as 'sleepy sickness' or 'Von Economo Disease', Encephalitis Lethargica is an especially devastating form of brain inflammation that eventually leaves the infected person in a catatonic state. Those that survive the disease are often left with a variety of brain damage, which may be noticed immediately or following a several-year period of latency. The second epidemic in question was the 1918 global influenza pandemic, which ultimately infected half a billion people. This particular strain of influenza was notable because most of the infected and deceased were healthy young adults, and not vulnerable children or elderly people. The unusual pattern of fatalities was attributed to the virus's ability to turn the body's own immune system on itself; those with the strongest immune systems faced the most severe cases of influenza. Survivors of serious cases of influenza often suffered tissue damage as a result of an autoimmune attack, and in some cases, the brain was affected. The two epidemics were not unrelated – both diseases are directly related to autoimmune reactions, and it has been suggested that one may give rise to the other.

When the influenza pandemic finally subsided in 1920, physicians noticed that some children who survived the epidemics suffered from a form of brain damage that was initially dubbed "Post-Encephalitic Behavior Disorder". The symptoms of this disorder correspond very closely with what we now know as Attention Deficit Hyperactivity Disorder, including short attention spans, lack of emotional control, reckless behavior and constant fidgeting. This was the first time in history that ADHD-like symptoms were connected, even speculatively, with underlying brain damage. This condition was initially dubbed 'Brain-Injured Child Syndrome'; the name was later changed to 'Minimal Brain Damage', before being amended to 'Minimal Brain Dysfunction'.

Since its first publication by the American Psychiatric Association in 1952, the Diagnostic and Statistical Manual of Mental Disorders, or DSM, has been treated as a definitive guide to the classification of mental disorders. ADHD was first entered into the second edition of the DSM in 1968, though at the time it was referred to as the 'Hyperkinetic Reaction of Childhood'. Psychologists soon realized that the disorder was not always manifested through hyperactivity, and so the third edition of the DSM, published in 1980, amended the name to Attention Deficit Disorder with or without hyperactivity, or ADD.

The first use of the term 'Attention Deficit Hyperactivity Disorder' appeared in the 1987 revision of the third edition of the DSM. The update officially made the term ADD obsolete, although much of the other information about the disorder was unchanged.

Sub-types of ADHD – predominantly inattentive, predominantly hyperactive and combined – were first recorded in the fourth edition of the DSM, which published in 1994. The information presented in this edition of the DSM remains current.

Causes of ADHD

Although ADHD is the most thoroughly studied child psychiatric disorder in existence, psychologists have not yet been able to pinpoint an exact cause for the disorder. They have, however, come up with several possibilities that may help to explain the root causes of the disorder.

One of the most striking differences between a normal brain and the brain of a person with ADHD is size: people with ADHD have significantly smaller brains than people without the disorder. In particular, the left side of the frontal cortex is much smaller than it is in a non-disordered person. Researchers have noted that many of the skills lacking in people with ADHD – including impulse control, careful decision-making, concentration and organization – are the responsibility of the left frontal cortex; the reduction in volume of the cortex alone may be a root cause of these ADHD symptoms.

Brain cells, or 'neurons', use special chemicals called neurotransmitters to communicate with one another and send messages throughout the brain. ADHD is primarily linked to decreased levels of a neurotransmitter called Dopamine. Dopamine is responsible for reward-driven learning in the body, and the release of Dopamine in the brain causes feelings of euphoria. Tourette 's syndrome, on the other hand, is believed to result from an excess of Dopamine in the brain. Despite their seemingly opposite physiologies, ADHD and Tourette's syndrome frequently co-occur in the same brain; the genetic reasons for the connection have not yet been uncovered.

Deficits in another neurotransmitter called Norepinephrine, which triggers the body's sympathetic nervous system to induce a 'fight-or-flight' reaction, may also be responsible for some symptoms of ADHD. Some research also suggests that people with ADHD may also have unusually low levels of Serotonin, which is a neurotransmitter that primarily regulates moods.

There is a great deal of evidence to suggest that ADHD is a genetic disorder. It has shown to be extremely heritable, and passes down from parents to children. An estimated 75% of all ADHD cases are linked to genetic components. Although the exact gene has yet to be pinpointed, it has long been noted that people with ADHD commonly display mutations in genes that code for dopamine transporters. A variation in one gene in particular, called LPHN3, is believed to be the root cause of roughly one in ten cases of ADHD. LPHN3 codes for a protein that assists with signal transduction, the process by which neurons in the brain communicate with one another, and people who possess the variant gene are particularly receptive to stimulant drugs which block neurons from reabsorbing the chemicals they use to send messages.

Another theory about the cause of ADHD points to the working memory. Working memory, colloquially referred to as "short term memory" is responsible for retaining and working with information as it is presented to the senses. Among other things, the working memory is capable of remembering sequences of words (including sentences, facts and lists), rehearsing information to be transferred to long-term memory, forming mental representations of visual images, and solving special problems, such as mentally going over a proposed driving route. The mental process that determines how much of the working memory should be devoted to a particular task is called the Executive Function. Tests have demonstrated that most people with ADHD struggle with tasks that require an efficient executive function, and performance is significantly worse than that seen in the general population. Roughly 80% of the ADHD population struggles with Executive Function Tasks, while only half of the general population has similar difficulties. But because Executive Function Problems are not a universal feature of ADHD, and because these problems remain relatively common in people without ADHD, executive function cannot be said to be a root cause of ADHD symptoms.

Certain prenatal conditions have also been proven to increase the risk of ADHD. Children of parents who smoke, and children born premature or at low birth weight have up to three times the normal risk of developing ADHD. Pregnant women should be careful to not smoke while pregnant, and to receive regular prenatal care to ensure a healthy birth weight. These birth conditions also increase the risk of Tourette's syndrome, along with the chances of the child having both ADHD and Tourette's.

Because ADHD consistently appears at rates above 1% in almost all populations, it must provide some sort of evolutionary benefit for the genes to continue to be selected. Anthropologists and psychologist theorize that early hunter-gatherer societies actually benefited from having individuals with ADHD. These individuals would have been less cautious and inhibited than the other people in the tribe, and would have quickly grown bored of routines, leading them to explore new areas and try new things. These early ADHD individuals may have been responsible for the discovery of new fertile lands and new food sources, making them attractive mates and allowing them to continue to pass on the genes for ADHD.

Comorbid Disorders

ADHD does not always occur on its own; it often appears simultaneously, or 'comorbidly' with other disorders. The most common disorders to occur comorbidly with ADHD are:

***Tourette's Syndrome*:**
As previously mentioned, Tourette's syndrome commonly co-occurs with ADHD. Over 90% of people with Tourette's syndrome have a second neurological disorder, and ADHD is the most common of those comorbid conditions.

The most notable symptom of Tourette's syndrome is the involuntary muscle movements or vocalizations known as "tics". Tourette's sufferers have at least one motor and at least one vocal tic occurring concurrently. Tics may be simple spasms or throat-clearing, or they may be complex, coordinated movements and utterances. Though Tourette's is popularly known for the uncontrollable cursing of some sufferers, this condition, called Coprolalia, appears in only one out of every ten Tourette's patients. Tics change throughout the course of the disorder; a person who suffered from an eye-blinking tic might eventually shift to a facial twitch or a hang-wringing tic. Tics also gradually shift in severity over time. Stressful or emotional events may trigger a particularly severe bout of tics, though this varies depending upon the individual. Tourette's syndrome sets in before age 18 – the disorder usually appears around the age of 10 – and tics must be present for over one year with no significant tic-free periods before a diagnosis can be made.

Like ADHD, Tourette's syndrome is a chronic condition with no known cure. Many adults find that their tics wane in severity and frequency as they age, though some experience no decrease in symptoms. Unlike ADHD, however, there are no effective treatments for Tourette's syndrome. Medications are available, but most patients choose to avoid them, as they have been found to cause a general "dulling" of the personality, and behavioral therapy has not been successful in eliminating tics. People with Tourette's syndrome are capable of suppressing their tics for a short time, but doing so requires conscious effort and results in great discomfort until tics are allowed to begin again. Fortunately, most cases of Tourette's are mild enough to permit normal work, school and personal life; and very few cases of the disorder are actually debilitating.

Oppositional Defiant Disorder:
Abbreviated as 'ODD', this disorder is found in up to one-half of all ADHD sufferers. ODD is characterized by stubbornness, willful disobedience, and hatred or mistrust of authority, and those with the disorder often blame others for their own mistakes and lash out violently over minor incidents. Children with ODD are extremely difficult to deal with, and often cause disruptions among their classmates and siblings. The presence of ADHD exaggerates ODD symptoms in children who suffer from both disorders. Some experts suggest that this is due to the impulsive traits shared by both disorders, while others believe that ODD symptoms may arise from the extreme frustration felt by many people with attention deficit disorders.

Children with both ODD and ADHD are more likely than usual to progress to the more severe conduct disorder, and around 50% of patients with comorbid ODD and ADHD eventually develop antisocial personality disorder.

Conduct Disorder:
One out of every five ADHD patients is found to suffer from Conduct Disorder. 50% of patients with comorbid ADHD

and ODD eventually go on to develop Conduct Disorder, which is twice the normal rate of progression for ODD alone. Conduct Disorder is a more severe form of anti-social disorder than ODD; the disorder is considered a precursor to anti-social personality disorder. Patients with Conduct Disorder show a callous disregard for societal norms and human rights. They also struggle with appropriate emotional displays, and many are incapable of showing empathy for other human beings. Roughly half of all children diagnosed with Conduct Disorder are also found to have ADHD.

Attention Deficit Hyperactivity Disorder is most strongly associated with the "child-onset" subtype of Conduct Disorder – symptoms generally appear before the age of ten. People with Child-Onset Conduct Disorder are the most severely affected by the disorder throughout their life spans, and they are far more likely to have serious neurological defects, problems at school, family difficulties, or aggressive and violent outbursts. Like ADHD, Conduct Disorder is three to four times more common in males than in females; this gender gap may be at least partially due to females' greater susceptibility to guilt. ADHD patients most at risk for developing Conduct Disorder are those who have IQs around one standard deviation below the mean; this generally corresponds to an IQ of 85. Children in deprived environments or dysfunctional families are also at a greater risk for developing Conduct Disorder.

Conduct Disorder is closely associated with illicit substance abuse. Virtually all youth with substance addictions display symptoms of Conduct Disorder. After recovery from addiction, half of these youth continue to show signs of Conduct Disorder.

Antisocial Personality Disorder:

18

Made famous by its association with serial killers, Antisocial Personality Disorder is a pattern of callous disregard for societal normal and human rights that persists throughout adulthood, causing problems with family and personal life. People with this disorder are often colloquially referred to as 'sociopaths'. Despite their similarities, psychopaths are diagnosed with slightly different criteria, and psychopathy is considered a separate affliction. An official diagnosis of Antisocial Personality Disorder can only be given once a person has reached the age of eighteen. Around half of all children who have comorbid ADHD and ODD, or ADHD and Conduct Disorder, will eventually be given this diagnosis. Individuals whose ADHD involves hyperactivity are at particularly high risk of developing conduct and Antisocial Personality Disorders. An individual's diagnosis with Antisocial Personality Disorder becomes evident when a person displays several of the following symptoms:

- Impulsivity
- Failure to learn from consequences
- Frequent lying or deception
- Pattern of violating social norms or laws
- Disregard for human safety
- Lack of remorse for actions
- Inability to meet any significant responsibilities
- Easily angered or driven to aggression

Antisocial Personality Disorder is comorbid with many of the same disorders as ADHD, including depression, substance abuse, anxiety and borderline personality disorder. ADHD shares many symptoms with Antisocial Personality Disorder, such as impulsiveness and irresponsibility, making it difficult to initially recognize both disorders in an individual. The two disorders likely spring from a common neurological defect or chemical imbalance, although it has been suggested that the frustration of ADHD exacerbates antisocial symptoms.

Sleep Disorders:

A variety of sleep disorders – notably Obstructive Sleep Apnea Syndrome – are common to people with ADHD. Exact numbers of ADHD patients suffering from sleep disorders are difficult to pin down, due to the wide variety of sleep disorders present, but initial estimates suggest that 50% of the ADHD population suffer from one sleep disorder or another. Obstructive Sleep Apnea Syndrome, one of the most common sleep disorders found among people with ADHD, occurs when an abnormally large tonsil or adenoids partially block up the airway, causing slow, shallow breathing, periodic stoppage in breathing and snoring throughout the course of sleep. An official diagnosis of sleep apnea can only be made in a sleep laboratory, and surgical interventions are available to eliminate the problem.

The consequences of sleep deprivation closely resemble the symptoms of ADHD – sleep-deprived children have difficulties concentrating, remembering important information, learning, attending to tasks and making decisions. Although sleep deprivation has not been shown to cause ADHD, it does exaggerate the symptoms, making the disorder much more difficult to manage.

Bipolar Disorder:

Around 20% of people with bipolar disorder also test positively for ADHD. Bipolar disorder is most commonly characterized by extreme mood swings, with 'highs' that consist of euphoria, reckless decision-making and extreme risk-taking, and 'lows' that consist of severe depression and suicidal thoughts. These manic or depressive episodes can last anywhere from a few hours to a few months, with periods of 'normal' behavior between them. The erratic behavior of a manic bipolar episode and the hyperactive behavior of ADHD are often confused for one another, making it extremely difficult to diagnose individuals who have both disorders. The connection between bipolar disorder and ADHD stems from a common brain defect and both are associated with a thinning of the brain's cortex.

Dyspraxia:
Characterized by a deficit in motor control, Dyspraxia affects many children that suffer from ADHD. The incidence of Dyspraxia in the population is around 6%, and as many as half of those with Dyspraxia also struggle with ADHD. Dyspraxia can affect speech, fine motor skills and general movement; usually, the disorder changes as a child ages. Young children will struggle to coordinate their general movements, and older children have difficulties with precise movements and language. In addition to motor control, Dyspraxia can also be detrimental to short-term memory, sensory processing and directional skills. Like ADHD, Dyspraxia is a chronic condition with no known cure. Having both Dyspraxia and ADHD seriously affects a child's classroom performance and children with these comorbid disorders should receive specialized help at school from a very early age.

Borderline Personality Disorder:
Known by the acronym BPD, or by the alternate name "emotionally unstable personality disorder, borderline type", borderline personality disorder is characterized by extreme emotions, impulsiveness, varying mood swings, unstable interpersonal relationships, and unbalanced self-image. Emotional episodes are longer and more intense in people with BPD than in people without the disorder, and emotional reactions to others' behavior are so extreme that a perceived slight or kindness can completely reverse a BPD sufferer's entire impression of another person. Their views towards

relationships are referred to as 'black-and-white thinking', as people with BPD tend to idolize and admire or mistrust and loathe a person, with few feelings in between. Perhaps unsurprisingly, those with BPD have extreme difficulty forming stable friendships or romantic relationships, and report frequent dissatisfaction with their partners.

Around one quarter of people with BPD also suffer from ADHD, which is roughly five times the normal rate of Attention Deficit Hyperactivity Disorder. Unfortunately, when the two disorders are comorbid, BPD is often overlooked, and ADHD alone is diagnosed. The medications used to treat ADHD can amplify BPD symptoms, and have even been known to cause psychotic episodes or paranoia. To prevent this, mild cases of comorbid ADHD are treated with behavioral therapy alone and severe cases of ADHD, that require medication, include anti-psychotic medication in the treatment plan.

Major Depressive Disorder:
Also known as MDD or 'clinical depression', Major Depressive Disorder involves a prolonged period of sadness, hopelessness and low-self esteem that takes a devastating toll on a person's relationships and home life. Sufferers lose interest in favorite activities and may begin to have suicidal thoughts. Up to one-third of all people who commit suicide in the United States each year were suffering from MDD. Initial onset of the disorder usually occurs between the ages of twenty and thirty, and the disorder can reoccur in an individual throughout the remainder of his or her life span. The condition is treated with a combination of antidepressant medication and psychotherapy.

Roughly one-third of all people diagnosed with ADHD will eventually develop major depressive disorder at some point in their lives. The biological link between major depressive disorder and ADHD is now believed to be a common gene mutation that affects calcium regulation in brain cells. Shared deficits in Serotonin, Dopamine and Norepinephrine pathways may also be to blame.

Like ADHD, Major Depressive Disorder is frequently comorbid with anxiety disorders and substance abuse.

Generalized Anxiety Disorder:
As the name suggests, Generalized Anxiety Disorder, or GAD, describes a condition in which a person is incapacitated by irrational worry far beyond what the average person would consider to be reasonable. Sufferers often obsess over remote possibilities of tragic events, such as the death of a loved one, health problems, money issues, interpersonal relationship collapse or work problems. In order to be diagnosed, this condition must persist for a minimum of six months and take a serious toll on the individual's day-to-day life. Currently, Generalized Anxiety Disorder is the most prevalent cause of work disability in the United States. Onset can occur at any time in the lifespan, although the disorder most commonly appears during early adolescence or in the early thirties. GAD is a product of both neurology and environment; the condition is most common in people who live high-stress lives, such as those below the poverty line, widowers, and the unemployed. Though GAD is twice as common in women as it is in men, the difference is attributed to women's increased rates of poverty, single parenthood and abuse, rather than any inherent biological difference between the sexes.

Approximately thirty to forty percent of ADHD sufferers have some form of anxiety disorder; GAD accounts for many of those cases. Oftentimes, the ADHD itself is the cause of anxiety; people with ADHD are prone to forgetting important deadlines and performing poorly on scholastic tests. The stimulant drugs often used to control ADHD symptoms can amplify anxiety, and so people with comorbid ADHD and GAD are often put on a combination of non-stimulant ADHD medications and anti-anxiety drugs.

Substance Abuse:
The term "substance abuse" refers to a situation wherein a person uses a psychoactive substance – such as drugs or alcohol – consistently in such a manner that prevents him or her from leading a normal life and attending to basic responsibilities. The dosages or methods of administration go against what is recommended by medical professionals or permitted by law. Addiction and dependency often become a factor in substance abuse. Exact specifications of what are considered to be substance abuse vary by legal jurisdiction. Antidepressants, therapy and rehabilitation clinics are all used to treat substance abuse problems.

People with ADHD are more likely to struggle with substance abuse than people without the disorder. Around a quarter of adults being treated for alcohol or drug addictions have ADHD; this is five times the rate of the general population. Youth are no exception. In fact, one study found that 14-year-old youth with ADHD were twice as likely to have started drinking as youth without ADHD. Those with ADHD are also more likely to use marijuana and to develop alcoholism.

The connection between ADHD and substance abuse can be partially attributed to the impulsive characteristics of the disorder. Sufferers are more likely to engage in a number of risky behaviors (drug use among them). ADHD may also share genes with the genetic risk factors for alcoholism, creating a biological connection between the two.

Despite concerns that the stimulants used to treat ADHD can themselves cause dependency, ADHD medications are not addictive if used in accordance with a prescription.

Chronic Bedwetting:
Primary nocturnal enuresis, commonly known as "bedwetting", is a condition that often accompanies ADHD. People with ADHD do not necessarily outgrow this bedwetting with time. It has been reported in ADHD patients well into their seventies. Persistent bedwetting can, in fact, be an early indication that a child has ADHD, and any child whose bedwetting problem persists should be evaluated by a psychologist for further signs of ADHD.

Diagnosing ADHD

A diagnosis of Attention Deficit Hyperactivity Disorder must be made by a licensed psychologist or psychiatrist. ADHD symptoms in children may be recognized by a parent, teacher or caregiver and any child suspected of having ADHD should be examined by a mental health professional as soon as possible. ADHD is often overlooked in childhood. Females, in particular, ADHD tends to manifest in less disruptive and destructive ways and any adult who displays ADHD symptoms should also make an appointment to be evaluated for the disorder.

When diagnosing ADHD, it is crucial that the inattentive or hyperactive symptoms be considered in multiple contexts, and not taken as proof of ADHD on their own. Many psychologists have made the mistake of evaluating children based on grade level instead of biological age. As a result, younger, less mature children are far more likely to be diagnosed with ADHD than their older, more developed classmates. An estimated one in five children diagnosed with ADHD is believed to have been misdiagnosed due to age.

In order to make a diagnosis of ADHD, it is essential that the inattentive or hyperactive symptoms have a negative effect on the individual's day-to-day life or general functioning. People whose symptoms appear to be consistent with ADHD, but do not cause any impairment in daily life will not be diagnosed with ADHD. Additionally, ADHD symptoms have to have appeared before the age of seven; symptoms that appeared after that time must be due to a different condition. The ADHD-like symptoms must also have been present in the individual for a minimum of six months before any assessment of ADHD can be made.

Symptom assessments are made using self-report questionnaires (for adolescents and adults), reports from parents and teachers, and direct observations made by psychologists. Several sets of guidelines for interpreting potential ADHD symptoms are available for mental health officials to use in making an official diagnosis.

The Diagnostic and Statistical Manual of Mental Disorders, commonly used in the United States as a guide for the diagnosing of mental disorders, requires that ADHD patients display several of the following inattentive and hyperactive symptoms:

- Forgetful
- Frequently daydreams
- Disorganization
- Easily distracted
- Difficulty completing tasks
- Inability to concentrate
- Restless
- Hyperactive
- Excessively fidgets
- Inability to sit still
- Impatience
- Destructive behavior
- Immature for age

Subtype of ADHD is determined by the distribution of symptoms in the inattentive or hyperactive categories. Children whose symptoms are roughly evenly divided between the two categories will be regarded as having the combined type of ADHD.

Even when sufficient symptoms are present for diagnosis, a psychologist must first rule out any alternative explanations for those symptoms. In adults, schizophrenia can cause most or all of the symptoms described by the DSM, and psychologists must rule out this disorder before they can carry through with a diagnosis of ADHD.

Another thing that psychologists must verify before making a diagnosis of ADHD is thyroid function. Hypothyroidism – in which the thyroid gland under-performs or does not function at all – can cause tiredness and fatigue, which in turn cause difficulties concentrating and avoiding distractions. Hypothyroidism is frequently mistaken for the predominantly inattentive form of ADHD. In contrast, hyperthyroidism – in which the thyroid gland over-performs – causes an excess of energy that is easily mistaken for hyperactivity.

Anemia (a lack of iron in the blood) and various sleep disorders can also cause fatigue in a child, preventing him or her from concentrating on schoolwork, remembering important information and tuning out distractions. Therefore, children suspected of having ADHD should be tested for these conditions before a diagnosis of Attention Deficit Hyperactivity Disorder can be finalized. Children suffering from undetected hearing or vision problems may also be mistakenly identified by teachers as having ADHD; being unable to hear instructions or read from a blackboard inhibits children from completing schoolwork, and it is crucial that these senses be regularly tested.

Children living in abusive households are also frequently mistaken for ADHD sufferers at school. Some children respond to abuse by acting out at school and engaging in destructive, attention-seeking behaviors, and may be mistaken by teachers as having the hyperactive form of ADHD. Other children deal with abuse by completely withdrawing within themselves, becoming unresponsive to

28

social or school environments. These children do not complete homework, fail to meet deadlines, lag behind their peers academically and generally do poorly at school. They may be incorrectly identified as belonging to the inattentive subtype of ADHD. Because ADHD sets in at very young ages, before children are able to properly verbalize or even recognize the abuse they face at home, it is important to examine the home lives of children that display ADHD symptoms at school before giving a diagnosis.

Socioeconomic status has also proven to be a factor in ADHD diagnosis. Children living in middle- or upper-class homes tend to be "over-diagnosed" – many children that do not actually have ADHD are mistakenly diagnosed. On the other hand, children growing up in working-class homes or impoverished conditions are often under-diagnosed. Oftentimes, children that do have ADHD do not receive the diagnosis or treatment they need. This discrepancy is attributed to differing standards of child behavior. Wealthy parents tend to set very strict standards for child behavior and academic performance, and children who achieve poor or average grades for a myriad of reasons are a cause for immediate concern. Upper- and middle-class families also have the financial resources to pay for appointments, expensive child psychologists, and other mental health professionals in order to seek a diagnosis; children with ordinary behavioral and disciplinary issues usually do not appear before psychologists, leading psychologists to overestimate the severity of their symptoms. Alternatively, some wealthy families have begun to intentionally seek a diagnosis of ADHD for children they know are healthy, in order to obtain special amenities on standardized tests and increase the chances of a child getting into a top university.

In lower-class homes, standards for behavior are often a lot less rigid than those found in wealthier households. Single-parent and dual-earning families are common, leaving children with little parental supervision from a young age. Academic performance is generally not as highly valued as it is in middle-class families, meaning many obvious signs of ADHD may be missed. Even at school, teachers may attribute poor behavior and grades to the children's underprivileged upbringing, missing the root cause of the problem. Costly child psychologists are generally inaccessible to poor families, making it difficult for their children to be properly diagnosed with ADHD.

ADHD Treatments

Although there is no 'cure' for ADHD, a number of treatments exist to help lessen and manage symptoms, allowing sufferers to lead relatively normal lives. Afflicted individuals may be treated with medications, behavioral therapy and changes in diet.

Medication is often the first course of action when treating ADHD. Roughly 80% of people with ADHD respond well to drug treatments and several safe, effective choices of medication are available. All ADHD medications fit into one of two categories: short-term and long-term acting. Short-term ADHD medications are fast-acting and last for only a few hours. These kinds of drugs must be taken two to three times a day, and are generally preferred for people with more severe ADHD who need precise control of their symptoms. The second variety, long-term ADHD medications, are taken in the mornings and generally last around twelve hours to provide relief from symptoms all day.

When starting drug therapy, regardless of the type or brand of drug, patients are started on extremely low doses of drugs. Gradually, over the course of several weeks, the dosage is increased until a dosage is found that manages symptoms with minimal side effects or discomfort. If a patient responds adversely to a low dose of a drug, or if a patient fails to respond to even a high dose of a drug, an alternative medication is found.

Medications are available in either stimulant or non-stimulant forms; the prior are generally based on amphetamines, or "speed". Though it seems counterintuitive, stimulants that would cause hyperactivity in a normal person actually have a calming and soothing effect on people with ADHD, allowing them to function normally in their day-to-day lives. Some people, however, cannot or will not take stimulants, and non-stimulant medication alternatives are available.

Generally, stimulants are the first choice for ADHD treatment, because they are known to be effective and because they work very quickly. Stimulants are safe for most children, though they are not given to children under the age of six. Regular use of any stimulant drug carries an inherent risk of stunted growth. This usually does not have a significant impact on adult height, but children on stimulants must still have their height and weight carefully monitored in case a problem should arise. Long-term stimulant use also carries the risk of a psychotic episode. If psychotic episodes should occur, patients may be given anti-psychotic medication or switched to a non-stimulant drug. Stimulant drugs used to treat ADHD include:

Ritalin –
The world 'Ritalin' has become practically synonymous with ADHD, and sure enough, Ritalin is one of the most popular ADHD medications on the market. It is also known by the generic name "Methylphenidate". Chemically and physiologically, Ritalin bears an extremely close resemblance to the street drug Cocaine, although it is much slower to take effect. It can take over an hour for Ritalin to noticeably raise levels of Dopamine in the brain, while cocaine achieves this in seconds. Ritalin works by amplifying quantities of Dopamine, Norepinephrine and Gluatamate in the brain, and so it should not be taken by persons with Glaucoma, severe anxiety or Tourette's syndrome, as it is dangerous to exacerbate those conditions with additional Dopamine. Ritalin can be addictive if taken improperly.

Common side effects of Ritalin include dizziness, headache, nausea, weight loss, insomnia, nervousness, loss of appetite and stomach pain. In rare cases, Ritalin can cause severe adverse reactions which include aggression, confusion, hostility, light headedness, easy bruising, numbness, changes in vision, increased heart rate, rash, blistering, migraines and extremely high blood pressure. Anyone suffering from an adverse reaction should seek immediate medical attention. Long-term use of Ritalin has been shown to stunt growth.

Ritalin should never be taken in conjunction with decongestants, blood thinners, blood pressure medications or certain common antidepressants, as dangerous drug reactions can occur. People using Ritalin should use extreme caution when driving or performing safety-sensitive tasks while on Ritalin, as the drug is known to impair decision-making processes.

The effects of Ritalin on a developing fetus are currently unknown. Thus, pregnant women are advised not to take it.

Adderall –

Perhaps one of the most well known of all ADHD medications, Adderall is made from a combination of four different Amphetamine Salts. Taken together, these Amphetamine Salts increase levels of the neurotransmitters Norepinephrine, Dopamine, and Serotonin in the brain.

The simultaneous increase of those three neurotransmitters – Dopamine in particular – helps to alleviate ADHD symptoms. The drug was formulated to address the neurotransmitter shortage in the brains of people with ADHD. Its stimulant properties also make it useful for treating narcolepsy, a condition that causes a person to spontaneously fall asleep at random times. Adderall, when used correctly, is currently one of the safest and most effective ADHD medications available, and many people who have had adverse reactions or become acclimated to Ritalin are switched to Adderall.

Mild side effects of Adderall include sweating, nervousness, weight loss, headaches, trembling and dizziness. Rare adverse reactions involving hair loss, bloody stools and loss of sex drive have also been reported. The effects of Adderall on a developing fetus are not well understood, though there may be a risk of low birth weight. Thus, women with ADHD are advised to stop taking Adderall while pregnant.

Concerta –
This is another brand name for the generic drug "Methylphenadate". It is identical to the drug, Ritalin.

Focalin –
In the generic form, this drug is sold as "Dexmethylphenadate", and it is extremely chemically similar to Methylphenadate, which is sold as Ritalin, Concerta and Methylin. Focalin is a Norepinephrine and Dopamine reuptake inhibitor. It prevents the cells of the brain from destroying the Norepinephrine and Dopamine they produce, enhancing the effects of these neurotransmitters. It is most active in the Limbic system at the striatum at the center of the brain. These structures are responsible for memory and emotions.

Because of its chemical similarity to Methylphenadate, side effects are identical to those seen in Ritalin. The drug is not to be taken in conjunction with Monoamine Oxidase inhibitors, as a fatal reaction may occur. Aside from ADHD, it is also used to treat narcolepsy and some cases of Major Depressive Disorder.

Dexedrine –

Like, Adderall, Dexedrine, or "Dextroamphetamine" is derived from Amphetamines. Dexedrine consists of the right-handed stereoisomer of Amphetamine, and it is the Amphetamine Salt that makes up three-quarters of a dose of Adderall. Dexedrine was used as an alertness agent long before it was used for medical purposes to treat ADHD. At one time, the drug was marketed to housewives who desired more energy for household chores and currently, it is used by the military to keep pilots and other personnel alert for long-haul flights. It was also widely issued to soldiers during the Vietnam War. The drug has been a controlled substance since 1970.

Dexedrine is an extremely potent ADHD drug with many unpleasant physical and psychological side effects. Possible side effects include:

- Dilated pupils
- Hyperactivity
- Tremors
- Heart palpitations
- Sweating
- Hypotension
- Hypertension
- Acne
- Twitching
- Numbness
- Pallor
- Diarrhea
- Constipation
- Tachycardia (rapid heart rate)
- Aggressiveness
- Increased libido
- Psychomotor agitation (unintentional movement)
- Dermatillomania (compulsive skin picking)

- Paranoia
- Hallucinations

Adverse reactions and overdoses can cause heart attack, stroke, rapid breathing, over responsive reflexes, confusion, panic and death. People who suffer from seizures, hyperthyroidism, glaucoma, hypertension, cardiovascular disease and arteriosclerosis are advised not to take Dexedrine.

Besides treating ADHD, Dexedrine is also used as a treatment for narcolepsy, Major Depressive Disorder and life-threatening cases of obesity. Experiments have also shown it to be effective in the treatment of fatigue and depression caused by cancer, HIV or severe stroke. Patients in physical therapy that take Dexedrine have been shown to recover movement much faster than those who are not taking the drug.

Vyvanse –
Known by the generic name "Lisdexamfetamine Dimesylate", Vyvanse consists of dextroamphetamine, or Dexedrine, in combination with the amino acide L-lysine in a 3:1 ratio. The drug is mostly used on children between the ages of six and twelve, and side effects are very similar to those of Dexedrine.

When not used to treat ADHD, Vyvanse has been used experimentally for the treatment of Major Depressive Disorder. It may also be effective at repairing cognitive functioning, and for use in the treatment of Schizophrenia, Binge Eating Disorder and excessive daytime sleepiness is being investigated.

Vyvanse is an extremely new drug on the market, and only received FDA approval for ADHD treatment in 2008, and approval for long-term usage in 2012.

Desipramine –
This drug works by blocking the brain's neurons from reabsorbing any of the neaurotransmitter Norepinephrine they release. It also partially blocks the reuptake of the neurotransmitter Serotonin. Norepinephrine is largely responsible for the sympathetic nervous system – the set of neural pathways that stimulate the fight-or-flight response – and blocking its reuptake also blocks pain signals from traveling from the spinal cord to the brain.

Because a lack of Norepinephrine is partially responsible for ADHD symptoms, increasing levels of the neurotransmitter with Desipramine can temporarily alleviate some ADHD-related traits. In particular, Desipramine has shown to be very effective for treating the frequent bed-wetting that often accompanies ADHD.

This drug is also used to treat recovering Cocaine addicts suffering from withdrawal symptoms. It has been linked to an increased risk of breast cancer in women.

Metadate –
This is another name for the generic drug "Methylphenadate". It can also be found under the names "Ritalin", "Methylin" and "Concerta".

Methylin –
This is yet another brand name for the drug "Methylphenadate". It is also sold under the names "Ritalin", "Metadate" and "Concerta".

Daytrana –

Unlike other ADHD medications, which are administered in pill form, Daytrana comes in the form of a medicinal patch. The drug – which was previously known as MethylPatch – is rarely prescribed at the time of an ADHD diagnosis. It is instead only used as a last resort when patients fail to respond to more traditional, orally-administered medications. The patch is meant to be worn for nine to twelve hours at a and it illegal to buy and sell them without a prescription. High demands for drugs like Ritalin and Adderall have driven up their street value, making it tempting for cash-strapped ADHD sufferers to begin selling their medications.

Schools have had a variety of reactions to the growing ADHD medication abuse crisis. Some are choosing to remind their students of the dangers of ADHD drug abuse; these stimulants are addictive if taken without a prescription, and long-term illicit use of these drugs can cause the development of mood disorders, aggression, irritability, high blood pressure, social withdrawal, cardiac arrhythmia, tremors, respiration difficulties and seizures. With sustained abuse, the drugs can cause strokes, hallucinations, paranoia, psychotic episodes, delusions and, ironically, difficulty concentrating. The dangers of unprescribed ADHD drug use are not limited to medical side effects. The drugs cause a euphoric state that impacts decision-making, leading some college students to engage in risky behaviors like unprotected sex, reckless driving and criminal behavior.

Other schools have chosen to wash their hands of the problem and have ceased to make ADHD diagnoses or dispense ADHD medications at on-campus health centers. This move has been widely criticized by educators and ADHD experts, who argue that it strips legitimate ADHD sufferers of much-needed resources, while not actually deterring students from abusing ADHD drugs. Many believe that cutting off access to stimulant drugs on-campus will merely drive students to seek the prescriptions they desire at other hospitals and medical clinics.

Parents of ADHD adolescents who are concerned about the possibility of their children selling off their medications should talk to their children about the legal and medical ramifications of stimulant abuse. It should be stressed to children from a young age that it is important to take drugs only as directed by a physician. Children should also be taught to resist peer pressure as there is a possibility that they will face direct requests for their medication. Personal safes and lockers can also be used to safeguard against medication theft.

Abuse by college students is not the only controversy surrounding stimulant ADHD mediations. Many parents are uncomfortable with the idea of their young children taking amphetamine-based medications, and some have voiced concerns that their children may be more likely to experiment with hard drugs in adolescence and adulthood. Longitudinal studies that followed ADHD patients for ten years to determine the validity of this claim found that use of stimulant medications did not make individuals any more or less likely to engage in illicit drug use. The drugs have consistently shown to be safe for even small children to use.

People that do not like the idea of being on stimulants and people with comorbid conditions that are agitated by stimulants may choose to take non-stimulant alternatives to treat their ADHD. Non-stimulants are thought to be less potent than their stimulant counterparts, though there is no reliable research to confirm this. Non-stimulant drugs that treat ADHD include:
time.

Stimulant ADHD medications have been the source of recent controversy on college campuses around the world. Many students, in a desperate attempt to boost their grades, have begun abusing ADHD drugs. When taken by people without ADHD, these drugs cause extended periods of wakefulness and alertness, allowing students to stay up for days on end to study and complete assignments. The weight loss side effects also make these drugs tempting for body-conscious students eating high-calorie diets at college. In an attempt to get the drugs, some students have begun faking ADHD symptoms to doctors and psychologists, in the hopes of being falsely diagnosed and given a prescription. Others have resorted to purchasing or stealing the drugs from friends and relatives who legitimately suffer from ADHD. Stimulant drugs are controlled substances,

Strattera: Also known as "Attentin" or by the generic name "Atomexetine", Strattera is a non-stimulant drug that inhibits the reuptake of Norepinephrine. The drug was known for years as "Tomoxetine", but had to undergo a name change to prevent pharmacies from confusing it with the breast cancer drug "Tamoxifen". Unlike stimulant drugs, Strattera is not addictive or subject to abuse by people without ADHD, and as such, is subject to fewer strict controls than Ritalin, Adderall and related medications. Originally, the drug was designed as a treatment for Major Depressive Disorder, but failed to provide any relief from depression in clinical trials.

Side effects of Strattera include nausea, dry mouth, irritability, hair loss, dizziness, sweating, sexual dysfunction, loss of libido, weight loss, hypertension, heart palpitations, increased heart rate, constipation, fatigue and painful or hesitant urination. Psychological side effects include suicidal thought patterns, self-harm, mood swings, psychosis, depression and mood disorders. In some people, long-term use may cause serious liver damage.

40

One of the advantages of Strattera is that it lasts for a twenty-four hour period, a feat that is simply not possible with stimulants. Because it is non-addictive, administration of Strattera may be stopped suddenly without weaning, though same patients report a dramatic increase of appetite and irregular bowel movements following discontinuation.

A 2010-2011 legal battle to make Strattera available as a generic was eventually settled in favor of the patent-holding company, Eli Lilly and Company. The drug is only available in brand-name form.

Wellbutrin:
Although it has not yet been approved for the treatment of ADHD, Wellbutrin, or "Bupropion" has been shown to significantly reduce hyperactive and inattentive symptoms in test trials. As an amphetamine substitute, Wellbutrin blocks brain cells from reabsorbing and destroying released Norepinephrine and Dopamine, thereby enhancing the effects of both of these neurotransmitters. Wellbutrin has a wide variety of clinical uses, and is sold under the following names:

- Voxra
- Zyban
- Budeprion
- Prexaton
- Aplenzin
- Elontril

Primarily, Welbutrin is used as an antidepressant and it is currently the fourth most widely used antidepressant in the United States. It is one of the only antidepressants available that does not cause sexual dysfunction, making it the drug of choice for people who have experienced a loss of libido with more popular drugs like Zoloft. It is also used to aid in the process of quitting smoking, as it significantly reduces symptoms of Nicotine withdrawal, including cravings for Nicotine. It is also commonly used to treat obesity. Real stimulants, though effective, have the unpleasant characteristic of being habit-forming, which Wellbutrin is non-addictive. It is also currently being tested for the treatment of social anxiety disorders and Agoraphobia (fearfulness of open spaces).

In addition to medication, many ADHD patients – particularly those with severe cases of the disorder – undergo a variety of therapies. The effectiveness of these therapies has not be scientifically researched, but anecdotal accounts by parents, teachers and affected individuals indicate that therapies do help to get symptoms under control.

Common psychotherapy, administered by a clinical psychologist, counseling psychologist or psychiatrist, is generally the behavioral treatment of choice. When used in conjunction with drugs, or even when used by itself, psychoptherapy has been consistently reported to be effective in managing inattentive and hyperactive behavior.

Other therapies are focused not on the afflicted individual, but on the parents – because ADHD has such a strong genetic component. The parents of ADHD children often display ADHD symptoms themselves, even if they do not have the full-blown disorder. Helping families to set up an environment that allows ADHD children to function more effectively is beneficial to the entire family. Children with ADHD require very structured sets of rules and expectations, and they can be operantly conditioned with rewards and punishments to complete schoolwork and refrain from destructive behavior. Even simple strategies, such as using a timer or stopwatch to track the amount of time spent on a task can dramatically reduce the amount of stalling and distractions experienced by children with ADHD.

Adults with ADHD can seek out specialized ADHD life coaches. These life coaches consider the type and severity of an individual's ADHD, and come up with realistic goals for work and personal achievements, along with appropriate strategies for achieving those goals. ADHD coaches are not certified by the American Psychological Association or the American Psychiatric Association, and should not be used as the sole course of treatment.

Although they have not yet been thoroughly researched, many "ADHD diets" exist that are intended to reduce ADHD symptoms. Connections between diet and the brain – and by extension, diet and mental health – are well established, and many psychologists agree that it is likely that diet plays some role in the manifestation of ADHD symptoms.

One of the most common dietary supplements recommended for those with ADHD is fish oil. Fish oil capsules provide omega-3 fatty acids, which are believed to boost concentration. Omega-3 fatty acids can also be obtained from other sources in the diet, such as cold-water fish, olives, canola oil, Brazil nuts and walnuts.

It is also recommended that those with ADHD eat a very high-protein diet. Protein is found in meat, fish, eggs, lentils, cheese, beans and nuts. For best results, protein should be eaten throughout the day, including breakfast and afternoon snacks. Protein is believed to improve the brain's ability to concentrate. Initial evidence also suggests that eating a high protein diet may increase the duration of the effects of ADHD medication.

People with ADHD may also benefit from removing simple carbohydrates from their diets and replacing them with complex carbohydrates. Simple carbohydrates, which are found in corn syrup, peeled potatoes, white flour, white sugar, white rice and honey, cause the blood sugar to quickly spike and then drop. This results in tiredness and difficulties concentrating. In contrast, complex carbohydrates keep blood sugar stable throughout the day and provide the energy needed for the brain to function optimally. Foods that contain complex carbohydrates include:

- Yams
- Apples
- Oranges
- Grapefruit
- Dill pickles
- Radishes
- Asparagus
- Strawberries
- Okra
- Onions
- Carrots
- Brown rice
- Barley
- Oats
- Buckwheat
- Corn
- Lentils
- Chick peas
- Kidney beans
- Soy milk

Daily multivitamins can also help to ensure optimum brain health and functioning. Some ADHD patients are too easily distracted to plan their nutrient intake or prepare healthy meals, and multivitamins can help to replace any vitamins that are accidentally missed from the diet. People with ADHD should be careful to avoid any nutrient deficiencies, and should consult with a doctor if they suspect they may be receiving inadequate quantities of particular vitamins and minerals. In addition, many vitamin supplements are available by prescription only.

In the mid-1970's, allergist Dr. Benjamin Feingold proposed that the consumption of artificial colorings, flavorings and preservatives may be responsible for triggering hyperactivity in children. His ideas have been controversial since their introduction, but many ADHD experts agree that children with Attention Deficit Hyperactivity Disorder should avoid these artificial food ingredients. In particular, red and yellow artificial food colorings should be avoided, as those seem to be most apt to produce hyperactivity.

The American Academy of Pediatrics also recommends that people with ADHD go out of their way to avoid consuming Aspartame, Sodium Benzoate, Monosodium Glutamate – commonly known by the acronym MSG – and Nitrites. Despite popular belief, sugar and small amounts of caffeine do not cause hyperactive behavior. There is a great deal of individual variation in foods that trigger hyperactivity so parents should closely monitor their children with ADHD to determine if anything in the child's diet seems to be causing hyperactivity. Keeping a food diary is an easy way to narrow down possibilities, and it will allow you to consult with a doctor if difficulties in pinpointing trigger food arise.

Daily exercise may also reduce hyperactivity and restlessness in people with ADHD. As little as twenty to thirty minutes of moderate physical activity each day can make a dramatic improvement in ADHD symptoms.